Start-Up

Connections

SEASIDE HOLIDAYS

Stewart Ross

Evans

First published in this edition in 2011
by Evans Brothers Limited
2A Portman Mansions
Chiltern Street
London W1U 6NR

Produced for Evans Brothers Limited by
White-Thomson Publishing Ltd.
+44 (0) 843 2087 460

Printed by New Era Printing Company Ltd. in Chai Wan,
Hong Kong, September 2011, Job number 1627

Editor: Anna Lee
Consultant: Norah Granger
Designer: Tessa Barwick

Cover (centre): tent-land at Hornsea, Humberside,
  circa 1910.
Cover (top left): on the beach at Margate, 1950s.
Cover (top right): children playing on beach, circa 1940.

British Library Cataloguing in Publication Data

Ross, Stewart
  Seaside holidays. - (Start-up history)
  1.Vacations - History - Juvenile literature
  2.Seaside resorts - History - Juvenile literature
  I.Title
  394.2'69'146

ISBN: 978 0 237 54421 8

Picture Acknowledgements: Corbis *(cover, top right)* 4, 6,
7, 14, 15 *(top)*, 18, 20; Hulton Getty *(cover, top left)*, 5 *(top)*,
8 *(bottom)*; Andrew Smith/Impact Photos 21; Mary Evans
Picture Library *(cover, centre)*, *(title page)*, 5 *(bottom)*,
10-11, 11, 15 *(bottom)*, 19 *(right)*, 19 *(left)*; Steve
Benbow/The Photolibrary Wales 8 *(top)*; Science and
Society Picture Library 9; Topham Picturepoint 12-13,
16-17.

VISIT OUR WEBSITE
Evans
www.evansbooks.co.uk

Contents

Seaside holidays now and in the past

These people are on holiday.
They are at the seaside.

holiday   seaside   years

► This family is on holiday 50 years ago.

▼ Here are people at the seaside almost 100 years ago.

How are their clothes different from today's clothes?

ago   clothes   different   today

January	February	March	April	May	June

winter   ⋯▸ spring

This is a timeline of a year.
These are the months of the year.
These are the seasons. ⋯⋯⋯

We have summer holidays in July and August.

What other holidays can you think of?

winter   spring   timeline   months

have holidays?

summer   autumn   winter

Some people
like to visit the
beach in **winter**.

seasons summer autumn beach **7**
......

How shall we get there?

▶ These people are arriving for a seaside holiday.

They have gone **abroad** by **plane**.

◀ This family is going to the seaside by **car**.

They will stay in their **caravan**.

abroad   plane   car

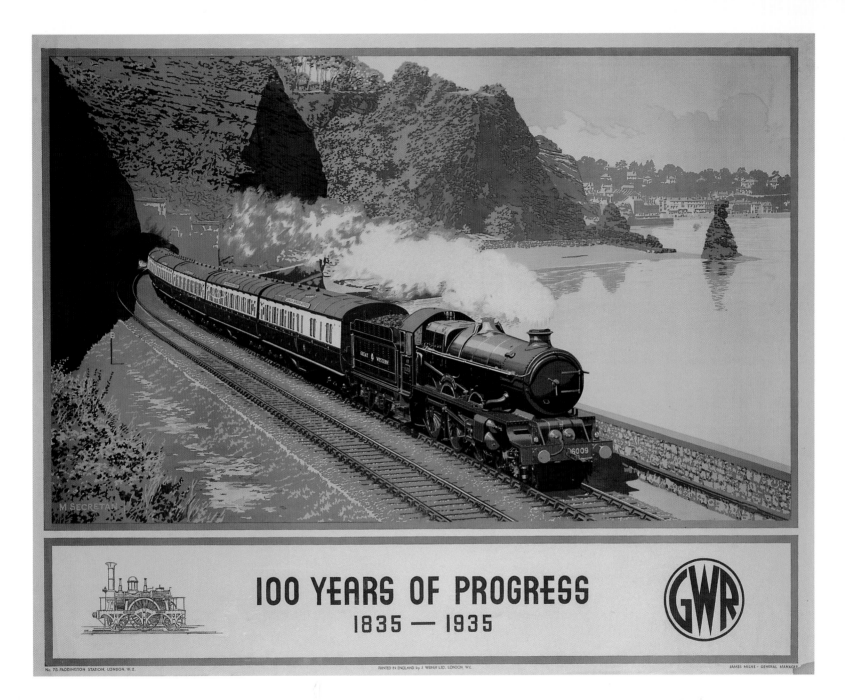

Long ago, steam engines pulled the trains.
The train in this poster is taking people to the seaside.

caravan   steam engines   poster   9

Hooray! We've arrived!

In the past,
people went to the seaside
in **buses** called **charabancs**.

How are these charabancs
different from buses today?

10

past   buses

Can you think
of some other ways
of going to the seaside?

charabancs

Looking at the past

What a crowded beach!
Is this a modern photograph?
Or was it taken long ago?

You can find out if you look at:

the pram

the food stalls

the men's hats

the women's dresses

modern   photograph

It is a
photograph of
Herne Bay
in Kent.
It was taken
almost 70 years
ago.

long ago   food stalls

Swimsuits now and then

These pictures are from different times in the past.

The most recent photograph was taken about 5 years ago.

recent

► **This photograph was taken about 60 years ago.**

◄ **The oldest photograph was taken about 70 years ago.**

How are the swimsuits on these pages different?

oldest   swimsuits   15

Fun at the seaside!

This photograph was taken about 100 years ago.

The people are listening to the band in the bandstand.

Find these things in the picture: houses, clothes, pier, sunshades, bicycles.

Which are the same as nowadays?

Which are different?

band   bandstand   pier

sunshades   **nowadays**

More fun at the seaside!

Here is a modern seaside ride.

ride   rollercoaster

► Here is a photograph of a wooden rollercoaster ride from 50 years ago.

▲ The photograph of this family playing cricket was taken about 80 years ago.

What seaside toys are in this picture?

cricket   toys

Punch and Judy

Here are two photographs of children watching Punch and Judy shows.

One was taken recently. One was taken in the past.

at the beach

What are the differences between them?

How are they the same?

Further information for Parents and Teachers

SEASIDE HOLIDAYS ACTIVITY PAGE

Use the activities on these pages to help you to make the most of *Seaside Holidays*.

Activities suggested on this page support progression in learning by consolidating and developing ideas from the book and helping the children to link the new concepts with their own experiences. Making these links is crucial in helping young children to engage with learning and to become lifelong learners.

Ideas on the next page develop essential skills for learning by suggesting ways of making links across the curriculum and in particular to literacy, personal development and ICT.

WORD PANEL

Check that the children know the meaning of each of these words from the book.

- abroad
- ago
- bandstand
- beach
- changed
- charabanc
- different
- holiday
- long ago
- modern
- month
- nowadays
- oldest
- past
- pier
- Punch and Judy
- recent
- same
- seaside
- season
- timeline
- times
- today
- years

PLANNING A PRETEND TRIP TO THE SEASIDE

1) Decide what to take

- Discuss what kinds of toys, clothes and entertainment you'd need to take.
- Children can write lists of what they would like to take. Ask them to take their lists home to see what can be provided from home.

2) Plan where your trip will take place.

- If possible, find an area of courtyard where you can place piles of sand for the children to play in. They can then paddle in a paddling pool.
- Alternatively, create a 'seaside' using small world people with sand and water.

3) Plan the picnic. What will you eat?

- Children can write shopping lists. Let each group of children research one type of food: sandwich fillings, flavours of crisps, type of juice, preferred fruit, preferred desert.
- Groups can make pictograms/ barcharts to show their results.
- If possible, take children to a shop in small groups to buy and pay for food for their picnic. Otherwise, provide the ingredients.

4) Enjoy your trip.

- Whether you take the children outside, or create the seaside in the classroom, allow children to wear their beach clothes and have their beach toys.
- If possible, follow the picnic with ice creams.

5) Don't forget the postcard!

- Take photographs of your seaside trip. Print them out and ask children to use the back as a postcard, writing to their family to tell them about the seaside trip.

FIND OUT MORE ABOUT JOBS AT THE SEASIDE

- Ask children to mind-map the kinds of jobs they think people might do in seaside towns. Encourage them to share their own experiences of holidays as well as exploring books.
- They could use a highlighter pen to identify all the jobs that were just the same 100 years ago. In a different colour, ask them to add in any jobs they things people did at the seaside 100 years ago which they don't do now.
- Consider why things might have changed at the seaside.

SAY CHEESE!

- Explain that in the past, photographers at the seaside would sometimes have seaside scenes painted with gaps in them. The seaside scenes included a funny looking person with a gap for a head. People put their faces in the gaps and had their picture taken. Find images on the internet to demonstrate.
- Challenge groups of children to plan and paint seaside pictures like this. They can paint people in modern clothes or clothes from long ago.

USING SEASIDE HOLIDAYS FOR CROSS CURRICULAR WORK

As citizens in 21st century Britain, it is important that children develop key competencies as
- successful learners
- confident individuals and
- responsible citizens.

Cross curricular work is particularly beneficial in developing the thinking and learning skills that contribute to building these competencies because it encourages children to make links, to transfer learning skills and to apply knowledge from one context to another. As importantly, cross curricular work can help children to understand how school work links to their daily lives. For many children, this is a key motivation in becoming a learner.

The web below indicates some areas for cross curricular study. Others may well come from your own class's engagement with the ideas in the book.

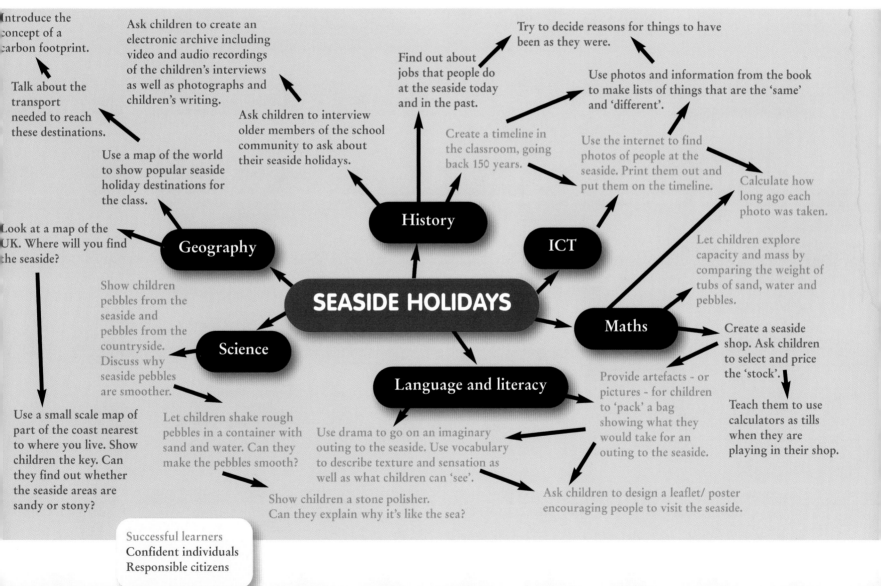

Introduce the concept of a carbon footprint.

Talk about the transport needed to reach these destinations.

Ask children to create an electronic archive including video and audio recordings of the children's interviews as well as photographs and children's writing.

Use a map of the world to show popular seaside holiday destinations for the class.

Ask children to interview older members of the school community to ask about their seaside holidays.

Find out about jobs that people do at the seaside today and in the past.

Try to decide reasons for things to have been as they were.

Use photos and information from the book to make lists of things that are the 'same' and 'different'.

Create a timeline in the classroom, going back 150 years.

Use the internet to find photos of people at the seaside. Print them out and put them on the timeline.

Calculate how long ago each photo was taken.

Look at a map of the UK. Where will you find the seaside?

Let children explore capacity and mass by comparing the weight of tubs of sand, water and pebbles.

Show children pebbles from the seaside and pebbles from the countryside. Discuss why seaside pebbles are smoother.

Create a seaside shop. Ask children to select and price the 'stock'.

Provide artefacts - or pictures - for children to 'pack' a bag showing what they would take for an outing to the seaside.

Teach them to use calculators as tills when they are playing in their shop.

Use a small scale map of part of the coast nearest to where you live. Show children the key. Can they find out whether the seaside areas are sandy or stony?

Let children shake rough pebbles in a container with sand and water. Can they make the pebbles smooth?

Use drama to go on an imaginary outing to the seaside. Use vocabulary to describe texture and sensation as well as what children can 'see'.

Ask children to design a leaflet/ poster encouraging people to visit the seaside.

Show children a stone polisher. Can they explain why it's like the sea?

History **ICT** **Geography** **SEASIDE HOLIDAYS** **Maths** **Science** **Language and literacy**

Successful learners
Confident individuals
Responsible citizens

23

Index